MW00337213

When I consider your heavens, the work of your fingers, the moon and the stars, which you have set in place, what is mankind that you are mindful of them?

PSALM 8:3–4 NIV

God has a wonderful plan for each person He has chosen.
He knew even before He created this world what beauty He would bring forth from our lives.

LOUISE B. WYLY

_I_ knew you before you were formed within your mother's womb; before you were born I sanctified you and appointed you as my spokesman to the world.

JEREMIAH 1:5 TLB

The moment you begin to delight in beauty, your heart and mind are raised.

BASIL HUME

May...God our Father, who loved us and by his grace gave us eternal encouragement and good hope, encourage your hearts and strengthen you in every good deed and word.
2 THESSALONIANS 2:16–17 NIV

I found loveliness today
Down along life's broad highway—
Beauty within pastures green,
Next in clouds of silvery sheen,
Golden glow at break of day,
Joy in children at their play.

CARLTON EVERETT KNOX

*W*alk into the fields and look at the wildflowers. They don't fuss with their appearance—but have you ever seen color and design quite like it?

LUKE 12:27 MSG

All that we have and are is one of the unique and never-to-be repeated ways God has chosen to express Himself in space and time.

BRENNAN MANNING

*W*e are His workmanship, created in Christ Jesus for good works,
which God prepared beforehand that we should walk in them.

EPHESIANS 2:10 NKJV

Far away, there in the sunshine, are my highest aspirations. I may not reach them but I can look up and see their beauty, believe in them, and try to follow where they lead.

LOUISA MAY ALCOTT

I will give you hidden treasures, riches stored in secret places,
so that you may know that I am the Lord.
ISAIAH 45:3 NIV

In the morning let our hearts gaze upon God's love and the love He has allowed us to share, and in the beauty of that vision, let us go forth to meet the day.

— ROY LESSIN

It is good to give thanks to the LORD and to sing praises to Your name,
O Most High; to declare Your lovingkindness in the morning and Your faithfulness by night.

PSALM 92:1–2 NASB

To share with a friend is to see twice the beauty.

Two are better than one, because they have a good return for their labor: If either of them falls down, one can help the other up.

ECCLESIASTES 4:9–10 NIV

The fountain of beauty is the heart, and every generous thought
illustrates the walls of your chamber.

FRANCIS QUARLES

Do not let kindness and truth leave you; Bind them around your neck,
write them on the tablet of your heart.

PROVERBS 3:3 NASB

As the moon reflects the sun, you, dear friend,
can light up the world as a mirror of God's goodness.

JENNIFER GERELDS

You're here to be light, bringing out the God-colors in the world.
MATTHEW 5:14 MSG

A woman of true beauty offers others the grace to be and the room to become.
JOHN AND STASI ELDREDGE

If your gift is to encourage others, be encouraging. If it is giving, give generously.... And if you have a gift for showing kindness to others, do it gladly.

ROMANS 12:8 NLT

He paints the lily of the field,
Perfumes each lily bell;
If He so loves the little flowers,
I know He loves me well.

MARIA STRAUS

For He will give His angels charge concerning you, to guard you in all your ways.
PSALM 91:11 NASB

The patterns of our days are always changing...rearranging...and each design for living is unique, graced with its own special beauty.

_____

_____

_____

_____

_____

_____

_____

_____

_____

_____

_____

_____

_____

_____

_____

_____

_____

_____

_____

_____

_____

_____

_____

_____

*A*ll the days ordained for me were written in your book before one of them came to be.

PSALM 139:16 NIV

All that is good, all that is true, all that is beautiful...be it great or small, be it perfect or fragmentary, natural as well as supernatural, moral as well as material, comes from God.

JOHN HENRY NEWMAN

Open your mouth and taste, open your eyes and see—how good God is.... Worship God if you want the best; worship opens doors to all His goodness.

PSALM 34:8–9 MSG

God cares for the world He created, from the rising of a nation to the falling of the sparrow. Everything in the world lies under the watchful gaze of His providential eyes.

KEN GIRE

Through the Lord's mercies we are not consumed, because His compassions fail not. They are new every morning; great is Your faithfulness.

LAMENTATIONS 3:22–23 NKJV

*The best things are nearest...light in your eyes, flowers at your feet,
duties at your hand, the path of God just before you.*
ROBERT LOUIS STEVENSON

You have made known to me the paths of life; you will fill me with joy in your presence.
ACTS 2:28 NIV

You are a creation of God unequaled anywhere in the universe....
Thank Him for yourself and then for all the rest of His glorious handiwork.

NORMAN VINCENT PEALE

The heavens declare His righteousness, and all the peoples see His glory.
PSALM 97:6 NKJV

Beauty is the radiance of truth, the fragrance of goodness.
VINCE MCNABB

Love and faithfulness meet together, righteousness and peace kiss each other.
Faithfulness springs forth from the earth, and righteousness looks down from heaven.

PSALM 85:10–11 NIV

The very act of planting a seed in the earth has in it to me something beautiful.
I always do it with a joy that is largely mixed with awe.

CELIA LAIGHTON THAXTER

It's not important who does the planting, or who does the watering. What's important is that God makes the seed grow.

I CORINTHIANS 3:7 NLT

In waiting we begin to get in touch with the rhythms of life—
stillness and action, listening and decision. They are the rhythms of God.

RICHARD J. FOSTER

_____

_____

_____

_____

_____

_____

_____

_____

_____

_____

_____

_____

_____

_____

_____

_____

_____

_____

_____

_____

_____

_____

How can we honor our GOD with our lives, the God who gives rain in both spring and autumn and maintains the rhythm of the seasons?

JEREMIAH 5:24 MSG

The splendor of the rose and the whiteness of the lily do not rob the little violet of its scent nor the daisy of its simple charm. If every tiny flower wanted to be a rose, spring would lose its loveliness.

THÉRÈSE OF LISIEUX

God has given each of you some special abilities; be sure to use them to help each other, passing on to others God's many kinds of blessings.

I PETER 4:10 TLB

All the world is an utterance of the Almighty. Its countless beauties,
its exquisite adaptations, all speak to you of Him.

PHILLIPS BROOKS

*W*orship the LORD in the beauty of holiness.
PSALM 96:9 NKJV

When one has once fully entered the realm of love, the world—no matter how imperfect—becomes rich and beautiful, for it consists solely of opportunities for love.

SØREN KIERKEGAARD

Sympathize with each other. Love each other as brothers and sisters. Be tenderhearted.
1 PETER 3:8 NLT

When life becomes difficult, when cracks spread through our existence and our strength seems to leak out, fill the gaps with hope. Like gold adorning distressed antique art, hope will reinforce, add value, and reveal more beauty.

BARBARA FARMER

God, pick up the pieces. Put me back together again. You are my praise!
JEREMIAH 17:14 MSG

When I need a dose of wonder I wait for a clear night and go look for the stars....
Often the wonder of the stars is enough to return me to God's loving grace.

MADELEINE L'ENGLE

_____
_____
_____
_____
_____
_____
_____
_____
_____
_____
_____
_____
_____
_____
_____
_____
_____
_____
_____
_____
_____
_____
_____
_____

He is the living God...his dominion will never end. He rescues and he saves;
he performs signs and wonders in the heavens and on the earth.

DANIEL 6:26–27 NIV

A fiery sunset, tiny pansies by the wayside, the sound of raindrops tapping on the roof—what extraordinary delight we find in the simple wonders of life!

WENDY MOORE

The whole earth is full of His glory.
ISAIAH 6:3 NKJV

As we grow in our capacities to see and enjoy the joys that God has placed in our lives, life becomes a glorious experience of discovering His endless wonders.

No eye has seen, no ear has heard, and no mind has imagined
what God has prepared for those who love him.

I CORINTHIANS 2:9 NLT

I still find each day too short for all the thoughts I want to think,
all the walks I want to take.... The longer I live, the more my mind dwells upon
the beauty and the wonder of the world.

JOHN BURROUGHS

I will show wonders in the heavens and in the earth.

JOEL 2:30 NKJV

The beauty of a woman is not in the clothes she wears,
The figure that she carries, or the way she combs her hair.
The beauty of a woman must be seen from in her eyes,
Because that is the doorway to her heart, the place where love resides.

AUDREY HEPBURN

_Charm is deceptive, and beauty is fleeting;
but a woman who fears the LORD is to be praised._
PROVERBS 31:30 NIV

Each one of us is God's special work of art. Through us, He teaches and inspires, delights and encourages, informs and uplifts all those who view our lives.

JONI EARECKSON TADA

I will give thanks to You, for I am fearfully and wonderfully made.
PSALM 139:14 NASB

*Life is so full of meaning and purpose, so full of beauty—
beneath its covering—that you will find earth but cloaks your heaven.*

FRÀ GIOVANNI GIOCONDO

The Spirit of God whets our appetite by giving us a taste of what's ahead. He puts a little of heaven in our hearts so that we'll never settle for less.

2 CORINTHIANS 5:1–5 MSG

Since love grows within you, so beauty grows. For love is the beauty of the soul.

AUGUSTINE

I have loved you with an everlasting love; I have drawn you with unfailing kindness.
JEREMIAH 31:3 NIV

God's holy beauty comes near you, like a spiritual scent, and it stirs your drowsing soul.

JOHN OF THE CROSS

So we are transfigured...our lives gradually becoming brighter and more beautiful as
God enters our lives and we become like Him.

2 CORINTHIANS 3:18 MSG

*Cheerfulness and contentment are great beautifiers
and are famous preservers of good looks.*
CHARLES DICKENS

I have learned the secret of being content in any and every situation....
I can do all this through him who gives me strength.

PHILIPPIANS 4:12–13 NIV

*In all ranks of life the human heart yearns for the beautiful;
and the beautiful things that God makes are His gift to all alike.*

HARRIET BEECHER STOWE

Every good gift and perfect gift is from above, coming down from the Father of the heavenly lights, who does not change like shifting shadows.

JAMES 1:17 NIV

The best and most beautiful things in the world cannot be seen or even touched.
They must be felt with the heart.
HELEN KELLER

*W*e fix our gaze on things that cannot be seen. For the things we see now will soon be gone, but the things we cannot see will last forever.

2 CORINTHIANS 4:18 NLT

*All God's glory and beauty come from within, and there He delights to dwell.
His visits there are frequent, His conversation sweet, His comforts refreshing,
His peace passing all understanding.*

THOMAS À KEMPIS

How precious to me are your thoughts, God! How vast is the sum of them!

PSALM 139:17 NIV

If we are cheerful and contented, all nature smiles...the flowers are more fragrant, the birds sing more sweetly, and the sun, moon, and stars all appear more beautiful, and seem to rejoice with us.

ORISON SWETT MARDEN

*A*nxiety weighs down the heart, but a kind word cheers it up.
PROVERBS 12:25 NIV

To appreciate beauty; to find the best in others; to give one's self;
to leave the world a little better...to know even one life has breathed easier
because you have lived.... This is to have succeeded.

RALPH WALDO EMERSON

Therefore encourage one another and build each other up, just as in fact you are doing.
1 THESSALONIANS 5:11 NIV

We will stand amazed to see the topside of the tapestry and how God beautifully embroidered each circumstance into a pattern for our good and His glory.

JONI EARECKSON TADA

He has made everything beautiful in its time.
ECCLESIASTES 3:11 NKJV

The beauty of the world about us is only according to what we ourselves bring to it.
BERTHA LINDSAY

You must each decide in your heart how much to give. And don't give reluctantly or in response to pressure. "For God loves a person who gives cheerfully."

2 CORINTHIANS 9:7 NLT

When God is involved, anything can happen.
God has a beautiful way of bringing good vibrations out of broken chords.

CHUCK SWINDOLL

We know that in all things God works for the good of those who love him,
who have been called according to his purpose.

ROMANS 8:28 NIV

One cannot collect all the beautiful shells on the beach.
One can collect only a few, and they are more beautiful if they are few.

ANNE MORROW LINDBERGH

_A_ pretentious, showy life is an empty life; a plain and simple life is a full life.

PROVERBS 13:7 MSG

*Nature is painting for us, day after day, pictures of infinite beauty,
if only we have the eyes to see them.*

JOHN RUSKIN

The whole earth is filled with awe at your wonders; where morning dawns,
where evening fades, you call forth songs of joy.

PSALM 65:8 NIV

In pageants, there is only one declared the fairest of them all. But with the Lord there is no competition. All have an equal privilege to have His image engraved upon their countenance. There is no truer beauty.

LYNN G. ROBBINS

Ah, you are beautiful, my love; ah, you are beautiful.
SONG OF SOLOMON 1:15 NRSV

Every year of my life I grow more convinced that it is wisest and best to fix our attention on the beautiful and the good.

RICHARD CECIL

*W*hatever is true, whatever is noble, whatever is right, whatever is pure, whatever is lovely, whatever is admirable—if anything is excellent or praiseworthy— think about such things.

PHILIPPIANS 4:8 NIV

God created me; that's why I'm here. He loves me; that's why Jesus died and rose again. He surrounded me with flowers and trees and birds and music and an array of goods, wanting me to have good things.

How great is the goodness you have stored up for those who fear you. You lavish it on those who come to you for protection, blessing them before the watching world.

PSALM 31:19 NLT

We live among marvels...each flower a masterpiece of subtle beauty, form, and scent.

MARION C. GARRETTY

You take care of the earth and water it.... The grasslands of the wilderness
become a lush pasture, and the hillsides blossom with joy.

PSALM 65:9, 12 NLT

It is one of the beautiful compensations in this life
that no one can sincerely try to help another without helping himself.

RALPH WALDO EMERSON

If you are generous with the hungry and start giving yourselves to the down-and-out, your lives will begin to glow in the darkness, your shadowed lives will be bathed in sunlight.

ISAIAH 58:10 MSG

The colored sunsets and starry heavens, the beautiful mountains and the shining seas, the fragrant woods and painted flowers, are not half so beautiful as a soul that is serving Jesus out of love.

FREDERICK W. FABER

There is a sweet, wholesome fragrance in our lives.
It is the fragrance of Christ within us.
2 CORINTHIANS 2:15–16 TLB

There are those rare moments in life when you are touched with so much love
that you begin to realize how beautiful life really is.

May you experience the love of Christ, though it is too great to understand fully. Then you will be made complete with all the fullness of life and power that comes from God.

EPHESIANS 3:19 NLT

Beauty born of beauty breeds beauty in every way.... A person who is given words of beauty is a person who will express beauty.... All beauty can be traced, ultimately, to God.

CHRISTOPHER DE VINCK

Let everything you say be good and helpful, so that your words
will be an encouragement to those who hear them.

EPHESIANS 4:29 NLT

In the central place of every heart, there is a recording chamber; so long as it receives messages of beauty, hope, cheer, and courage, so long you are young.

DOUGLAS MACARTHUR

One thing I ask from the LORD, this only do I seek: that I may dwell in the house of the LORD
all the days of my life, to gaze on the beauty of the LORD.

PSALM 27:4 NIV

For attractive lips, speak words of kindness.
For lovely eyes, seek out the good in people.
For a slim figure, share your food with the hungry.

SAM LEVENSON

She opens her arms to the poor and extends her hands to the needy....
She is clothed with strength and dignity; she can laugh at the days to come. She speaks
with wisdom, and faithful instruction is on her tongue.

PROVERBS 31:20, 25–26 NIV

Beauty puts a face on God. When we gaze at nature, at a loved one, at a work of art, our soul immediately recognizes and is drawn to the face of God.

MARGARET BROWNLEY

Just as each day brims with your beauty, my mouth brims with praise.

PSALM 71:8 MSG

Some days, it is enough encouragement just to watch the clouds break up and disappear, leaving behind a blue patch of sky and bright sunshine that is so warm upon my face. It's a glimpse of divinity; a kiss from heaven.

*Everything in the heavens and on earth is yours, O LORD,
and this is your kingdom. We adore you as the one who is over all things.*
1 CHRONICLES 29:11 NLT

*W*omen are beautiful, every single one of us.
It is one of the glorious ways that we bear the image of God.

STASI ELDREDGE

_____

_____

_____

_____

_____

_____

_____

_____

_____

_____

_____

_____

_____

_____

_____

_____

_____

_____

_____

_____

_____

_____

_____

_____

_____

Be beautiful inside, in your hearts, with the lasting charm
of a gentle and quiet spirit that is so precious to God.

I PETER 3:4 TLB

Go outside, to the fields, enjoy nature and the sunshine,
go out and try to recapture happiness in yourself and in God.
Think of all the beauty that's still left in and around you and be happy!

ANNE FRANK

How precious to me are your thoughts, God! How vast is the sum of them!
Were I to count them, they would outnumber the grains of sand.
PSALM 139:17–18 NIV

The beauty of the earth, the beauty of the sky, the order of the stars, the sun, the moon...their very loveliness is their confession of God: for who made these lovely mutable things, but He who is Himself unchangeable beauty?

AUGUSTINE

*Praise him, sun and moon; praise him, all you shining stars. Praise him,
you highest heavens.... Let them praise the name of the LORD,
for at his command they were created.*

PSALM 148:3–5 NIV

Don't ever let yourself get so busy that you miss those little but important extras in life—the beauty of a day...the smile of a friend...the serenity of a quiet moment alone.

*W*here you are right now is God's place for you.
Live and obey and love and believe right there.

In everyone's heart there is a secret nerve that answers to the vibrations of beauty.
CHRISTOPHER MORLEY

He has planted eternity in the human heart.

ECCLESIASTES 3:11 NLT

*O*ur Creator would never have made such lovely days, and given us the deep hearts to enjoy them, above and beyond all thought, unless we were meant to be immortal.

NATHANIEL HAWTHORNE

O L ORD, what a variety of things you have made! In wisdom you have made them all.
PSALM 104:24 NLT

Though I have seen the oceans and mountains, though I have read great books and seen great works of art...there is nothing greater or more beautiful than those people I love.

CHRISTOPHER DE VINCK

Dear brothers and sisters, we can't help but thank God for you, because your faith
is flourishing and your love for one another is growing.

2 THESSALONIANS 1:3 NLT

Just when we think...that our lives are nothing but heaps of ashes,
God pours His living water over us and mixes the ashes into clay.
He then takes this clay and molds it into a vessel of beauty.

LYSA TERKEURST

You, Lord, are our Father. We are the clay, you are the potter;
we are all the work of your hand.

ISAIAH 64:8 NIV

How beautiful a day can be when kindness touches it.

GEORGE ELLISTON

May the Lord cause you to increase and abound in love for one another,
and for all people.
1 THESSALONIANS 3:12 NASB

Above all give me grace to use these beauties of earth without me
and this eager stirring of life within me as a means whereby my soul may
rise from creature to Creator, and from nature to nature's God.

JOHN BAILLIE

*W*hom have I in heaven but you? And there is nothing on earth that
I desire other than you. My flesh and my heart may fail, but God is the strength
of my heart and my portion forever.

PSALM 73:25–26 NRSV

It is the simple things of life that make living worthwhile, the sweet fundamental things
such as love and duty, work and rest, and living close to nature.

LAURA INGALLS WILDER

*W*e brought nothing into the world, and we can take nothing out of it.
But if we have food and clothing, we will be content with that.

I TIMOTHY 6:7–8 NIV

In the sun's light, we catch warm rays of grace and glimpse God's eternal design.
In the birds' song, we hear His voice and it reawakens our desire for Him.
At the wind's touch, we feel His Spirit and sense our eternal existence.

WENDY MOORE

$\mathcal{O}$ LORD my God, how great you are!.... You stretch out the starry curtain
of the heavens.... You make the clouds your chariot; you ride upon the wings of the wind.

PSALM 104:1-3 NLT

The world rings with praise.... I think we delight to praise what we enjoy because the praise not merely expresses but completes the enjoyment; it is the appointed consummation.

C. S. LEWIS

You will go out in joy and be led forth in peace; the mountains and hills will burst into song before you, and all the trees of the field will clap their hands.

ISAIAH 55:12 NIV

All this beauty exists so you and I can see [God's] glory, His artwork.
It's like an invitation to worship Him, to know Him.

DONALD MILLER

Honor the Lord for the glory of his name.
Worship the Lord in the splendor of his holiness.
PSALM 29:2 NLT

We need to recapture the power of imagination;
we shall find that life can be full of wonder, mystery, beauty, and joy.

SIR HAROLD SPENCER JONES

God can do anything, you know—far more than you could ever imagine
or guess or request in your wildest dreams! He does it...by working within us,
his Spirit deeply and gently within us.

EPHESIANS 3:20–21 MSG

Thank You, Lord, for the grace of Your love, for the grace of friendship,
and for the grace of beauty.
HENRI J. M. NOUWEN

All things are for your sakes, that grace...may cause thanksgiving
to abound to the glory of God.
2 CORINTHIANS 4:15 NKJV

I often think flowers are the angels' alphabet whereby they write on hills and fields mysterious and beautiful lessons for us to feel and learn.

LOUISA MAY ALCOTT

Praise him, all his angels; praise him, all his heavenly hosts. Praise him, sun and moon; praise him, all you shining stars.... Praise the LORD from the earth... you mountains and all hills.

PSALM 148:2–3, 7, 9 NIV

My friends have made the story of my life. In a thousand ways
they have turned my limitations into beautiful privileges.

HELEN KELLER

Friends love through all kinds of weather, and families stick together in all kinds of trouble.
PROVERBS 17:17 MSG

God, the master artist...wants to paint a beautiful portrait of His Son
in and through your life. A painting like no other in all of time.

JONI EARECKSON TADA

I pray that God, the source of hope, will fill you completely with joy and peace because you trust in him. Then you will overflow with confident hope through the power of the Holy Spirit.

ROMANS 15:13 NLT

Flowers never emit so sweet and strong a fragrance as before a storm. Beauteous soul! when a storm approaches thee, be as fragrant as a sweet-smelling flower.

JEAN PAUL RICHTER

There is wonderful joy ahead, even though you have to endure many trials
for a little while. These trials will show that your faith is genuine.

1 PETER 1:6–7 NLT

Lord, give me an open heart to find You everywhere, to glimpse the heaven enfolded in a bud, and to experience eternity in the smallest act of love.

MOTHER TERESA

Let us consider how we may spur one another on toward love and good deeds.

HEBREWS 10:24 NIV

Everybody needs beauty as well as bread, places to play in and pray in,
where nature may heal and give strength to body and soul.
JOHN MUIR

Dear friend, I pray that you may enjoy good health and that all may go well with you,
even as your soul is getting along well.
3 JOHN 1:2 NIV

Ellie Claire™ Gift & Paper Expressions
Brentwood, TN 37027
EllieClaire.com

BeYOUtiful Journal
© 2014 by Ellie Claire, an imprint of Worthy Media, Inc.

ISBN 978-1-60936-934-7

Stock or custom editions of Ellie Claire titles may be purchased in bulk for educational, business, ministry, fundraising, or sales promotional use. For information, please e-mail info@EllieClaire.com

Compiled by Barbara Farmer

Printed in China

1 2 3 4 5 6 7 8 9 – 19 18 17 16 15 14